Ruth
THE HARVEST GIRL

The Story of Ruth
accurately retold from the Bible by
CARINE MACKENZIE

Design and Illustrations
Mackay Design Associates Ltd

Published in Great Britain by
CHRISTIAN FOCUS PUBLICATIONS LTD
Geanies House, Fearn, Tain, Ross-shire IV20 1TW, Scotland
© 1980 Christian Focus Publications. ISBN 0 906731 07 0
B/G 3-8

Reprint 1984

Published in Australia and New Zealand by
DAYSTAR *and distributed by* W. A. BUCHANAN & CO
21 Kyabra Street, Fortitude Valley, Brisbane, Q, Australia 4006
© 1984 Daystar ISBN 0 949925 12 8

Now translated into Dutch, French, Gaelic, German, Italian,
Norwegian, Spanish, Swedish, Welsh

Long ago, in the land of Moab,
there lived a girl called Ruth.

Ruth did not know or worship God.
She and her family worshipped
idols, as the people of Moab did.

At the same time, far away in the
town of Bethlehem, in the land of
Israel, there lived another family.
There was father Elimelech,
mother Naomi and their two boys,
Mahlon and Chilion. They
worshipped God.

Although they worked hard on their farm they did not have enough food, because there was a famine in the country.

Elimelech was very worried, so he took his family to the land of Moab, where there was no famine.

After some time, great sadness came to this family. Elimelech died. Poor Naomi was now a widow, and her two sons were without a father.

Mahlon and Chilion grew up and married Moabite girls. Chilion's wife was called Orpah; but who was the girl who became the wife of Mahlon? It was Ruth!

After Ruth married Mahlon, she stopped worshipping the false gods of Moab. She began to trust in the true God and to worship Him.

Later on, more sorrow came to the family. Mahlon and Chilion died also.

What a sad little family it was now, with no men to look after it and to do the farm work.

Naomi was many miles away from her friends who could help her.

One day, Naomi said to Ruth and Orpah, "I must go back to Bethlehem. I have heard that there is plenty food there now." She set off for Bethlehem and Ruth and Orpah went with her.

After they had gone some distance, Naomi said to the girls, "You have come far enough. Go back to your own people now. I hope you get married again soon. May the Lord bless you, for you have been so kind to me."

Then Naomi kissed them and they
both wept.
"We do not want to leave you,"
said Ruth and Orpah. "We love
you so much. We must go with
you."

Naomi kept telling them to go back. Orpah then changed her mind and decided that she would go back to stay in Moab after all. She kissed Naomi and said goodbye; but Ruth clung to Naomi.

Then Naomi said to Ruth, "Orpah is going back to her own people. You go with her now."

But Ruth would not go. She said to Naomi, "Please do not tell me to leave you. I will go wherever you go. I will live where you live. Your people will be my people, and your God will be my God."

Ruth chose to follow God and to be with God's people. Would you make the same choice as Ruth?

When Naomi saw that Ruth was really determined to stay with her, she did not ask her again to go back to Moab.

Ruth and Naomi travelled on until
they came to Bethlehem. The
news of their arrival spread quickly
among the people of the town.
Many of them remembered Naomi
and her family and they came to
see if this was really Naomi.

Ruth and Naomi arrived in
Bethlehem at the beginning of
harvest time. Poor people, like
them, were allowed to glean or
gather up the grain that the
harvest workers, or reapers,
dropped and left behind.

One morning, Ruth asked Naomi, "May I go to glean in one of the fields today?" Ruth hoped to bring home some barley to make bread. Naomi encouraged her to go.

Ruth went into one of the harvest
fields. She did not know who
owned the field, but God had
guided her into the field of a good
man called Boaz, who was famous
and rich. God is able to guide us
also.

During the day Boaz came to see
how his reapers were getting on.
He noticed Ruth working and then
asked the man in charge of the
reapers, "Who is that girl over
there?"

"That is the girl from Moab who came back with Naomi," the man replied. "She came to me this morning and asked if she could glean some barley. She has been busy from early morning until now."

Boaz went over to Ruth and spoke kindly to her. "Do not go to any other field to glean," he said. "Stay beside my girls. When you are thirsty, help yourself to our water."

Ruth was very surprised and grateful and she asked him, "Why are you so kind to me when I am just a stranger?"

"I have heard how kind you have been to Naomi," Boaz replied, "and how you left your own people to come with her. You have come to trust in the Lord God and may He reward you."

Ruth then thanked Boaz for being so kind to her.

Boaz showed Ruth even more kindness. He told her to sit beside the reapers at mealtimes and share their food.

Boaz quietly told his men, "Let Ruth glean anywhere in the field. You must drop some handfuls of barley specially for her to gather."

By evening, Ruth was feeling very tired, but she was pleased with her day's work. Before she went home, she beat the heads of the barley to remove the grain, and she carried home a large basket full of grain.

Naomi was thrilled to hear that Ruth had been in the field of Boaz all day. "Boaz is a good man," she said to Ruth, "and he is related to my husband. You should stay in his fields for the rest of the harvest."

Ruth did as Naomi said and so they had some food; but what would they do when it was finished? Both Ruth and Naomi were poor widows.

"I would love to see you happily married again," Naomi said to Ruth one day. "You know that by our laws, Mahlon's closest relative should marry you and look after you. He could also buy back or redeem our land. Boaz is a very close relative. I believe he would help you."

Naomi then told Ruth what to do. "You must go to Boaz tonight. He will be in the barn where they thresh the grain. Ask him to redeem the land; but do not speak to him until after he has gone to rest."

Ruth did just as Naomi had said.
She waited until it was dark and
Boaz was resting.

Boaz got quite a fright when he discovered a woman in the barn. When he knew who she was and what she wanted he said, "I would gladly redeem your land, but there is a relative who is closer to you than I am. He must be asked before me. I will ask him tomorrow morning. If he will not help you then I will help you."

Ruth went home early in the morning, before anyone else was awake. She did not go home empty-handed, for Boaz gave her a large amount of barley to take to Naomi.

Ruth told Naomi what had happened. Naomi said, "Do not worry any more, Ruth. Everything will be settled before the end of the day."

That day Boaz went to the gate of
the town, where people often met,
and found his relative there.

Boaz asked him, "Are you willing
to redeem Naomi's land? If you
cannot, then I will have to, for I am
next in line after you."

The man replied, "I will redeem it."

Then Boaz said, "If you redeem
the land you must also marry
Ruth, the widow of Mahlon."

"Oh no," answered the man, "I
cannot do that. You may redeem
the land for yourself."

The man took off his shoe and gave it to Boaz. This was the special sign to show that the matter was settled and that Boaz now had the right to redeem.

Boaz was delighted. He turned to the people, who had gathered round to listen. "You have heard that," he said. "I now have the right to buy the land that belonged to Elimelech and his son. I have the right also to marry Ruth, the widow of Mahlon."

Everybody agreed. They wished Boaz and Ruth every blessing in their marriage.

Ruth and Boaz were soon married.
God gave them the gift of a baby
son, whom they called Obed. How
delighted they were!

Naomi also was full of joy, for she
now had a little boy in her home
once more.

So we see that God was ruling in Ruth's life, as He does in your life and mine; and that He provided for Ruth and Naomi in a most wonderful way.

Ruth's baby was an important baby because he became the grandfather of the great king, David, who wrote most of the lovely psalms in the Bible.

But the most important descendant of Boaz and Ruth was the Lord Jesus Christ, who was born in the same town, Bethlehem, many years later.

Boaz was a redeemer for Ruth. So Jesus Christ is the Redeemer of His people. The redemption payment which Jesus gave was His own life, so that many sinners could be forgiven and become His people.